Succeeding at SATS

NATIONAL CURRICULUM
SCIENCE

Your guide to the KS2 National Curriculum Tests

Jill Dahlhoff

Collins*Children's*Books
Copyright © HarperCollins Publishers Ltd 1997

Note for Pupils

What do the Key Stage 2 National Tests mean to you?

The tests help you check your progress in **English**, **Science** and **Mathematics** through Key Stage 2. By assessing your strengths and weaknesses they enable you to set your targets for future progress in these subjects. Your teachers will send the results of your test to your secondary school to help them decide the best subject group for you.

When will you take these tests?

They take place in May of each year.

What do the Science National Tests consist of?

- The tests are divided into 2 main parts: Tests A and B. They are both of equal standard.
- Both tests will take 35 minutes each.
- The tests set questions to see how well you understand the four main parts of the curriculum for Key Stage 2. These are: Experimental and Investigative Science; Life Processes and Living Things; Materials and Properties; Physical Processes.
- You will find that this book does not cover every area on which you may be tested. The questions are selected from the curriculum and have been designed to to be as close as possible to the type of questions you will be asked.

What is a level?

While at school you will have the chance to progress through 8 levels in each subject. By the end of Key Stage 2 you should expect to be between levels 3 and 5. The results give the level you can expect to be placed in for each subject.

What does this book do for you?

- It shows the layout of the tests, and the types of questions you can expect.
- It shows you how to follow instructions precisely.
- It gives you practice in writing the test, and the confidence that comes with preparation.
- It shows you how to assess your own answers.

How to use this book

Get an adult to read through the instructions for each section with you, and to tell you when to start and finish the test. They should help you to assess your answers and determine your approximate level.

Equipment you will need

You will need the following equipment for answering the questions:
- a pen, pencil and rubber
- a ruler (30 cm plastic ruler is most suitable)
- a calculator (one with four functions is all you require)
- an angle-measurer
- tracing paper
- a mirror

You may **not** use a calculator in Test A.
You may use one in Test B.

Top Tips

- Tackle each question. **No answer means no marks.**
- Be sure to do exactly as you are instructed. So if asked to tick a box do so. Don't ring it or cross it out.
- If you do want to cross something out, do it clearly. There must be no doubt about what you intend your answer to be.
- **Don't panic.** If you practise in your weaker areas you'll be ready for the real test.
- With an adult use the boxes in the margin of the test papers to insert the marks you have awarded yourself. Write a total at the bottom of the page, and transfer the totals to page 48.

Tests A and B

Instructions

1) You have 35 minutes for Test A and 35 minutes for Test B. If you don't finish in time, make a note of how far you are, and continue working.

2) Read the questions very carefully.

3) The questions for you to answer are in tinted boxes.

4) If you don't understand a word you can ask an adult to explain it to you, providing it isn't a scientific word. For example, the word 'describe' may be explained, but not 'condensation'.

5) Try to do all the questions. If you find a question you can't do, leave it and return to it later.

6) Spaces and lines are provided for the answers. These give an indication of how much to write. It is best though, to keep answers fairly short.

7) You may be asked to:
- add to a diagram
- draw a new diagram.

These should be done as neatly and as clearly as you can.

8) If you want to cross out, do it clearly. There must be no doubt what the answer is.

9) If asked to **tick** a box, do so. Don't circle or underline. If asked to tick **three** boxes, don't tick more than three.

Test A

Materials

1

The plastic bottle has oil in it.

Write in the three boxes below to show the parts which are:

| solid | liquid | gas |

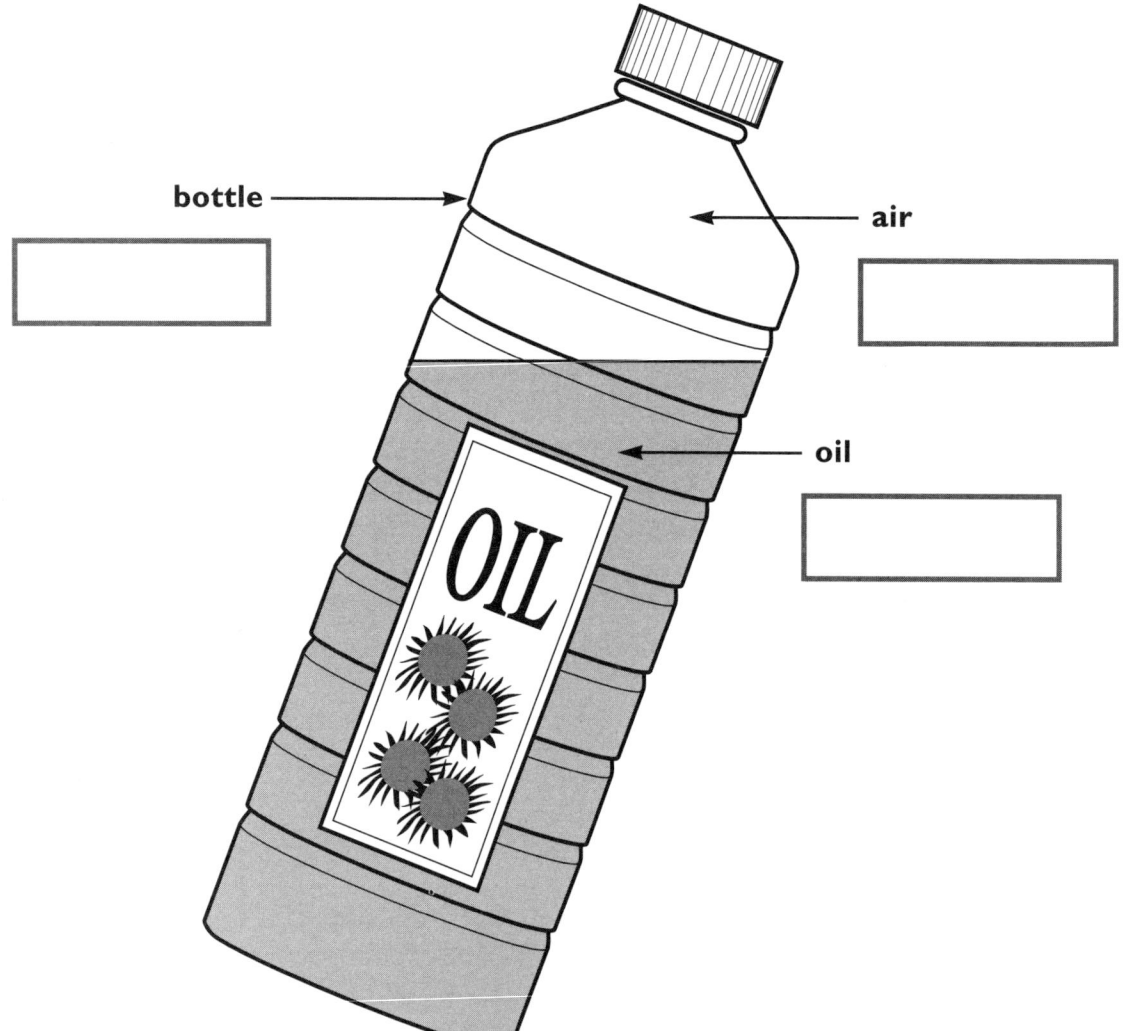

bottle →

← air

← oil

3

total

Magnets

Pippa is playing with two plastic toy dogs. They have magnets at their nose and tails. She puts them like this:

They stick together.

a) Name the **force** that causes them to stick together.

_____

She tries one dog a different way:

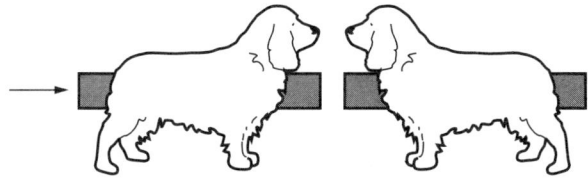

b) What happens as she **moves them together**?

_____

c) Say **why** this happens.

_____
_____

Any magnet on the toy dogs will stick to **one** of the objects shown below.

copper bracelet　　　gold ring　　　steel can　　　silver coin

d) Which one?

_____

Sound

3

Helena is playing the guitar. To play a guitar, the strings have to be plucked.

a) Explain **why the strings make a sound** when they are **plucked**.

_____

The strings have different thicknesses.

b) Which string would make the **lowest** note?

_____

c) How could you make **this string** make a **higher** note?

_____
_____

Human Body

4

stomach   kidneys   lungs   heart   brain   intestines

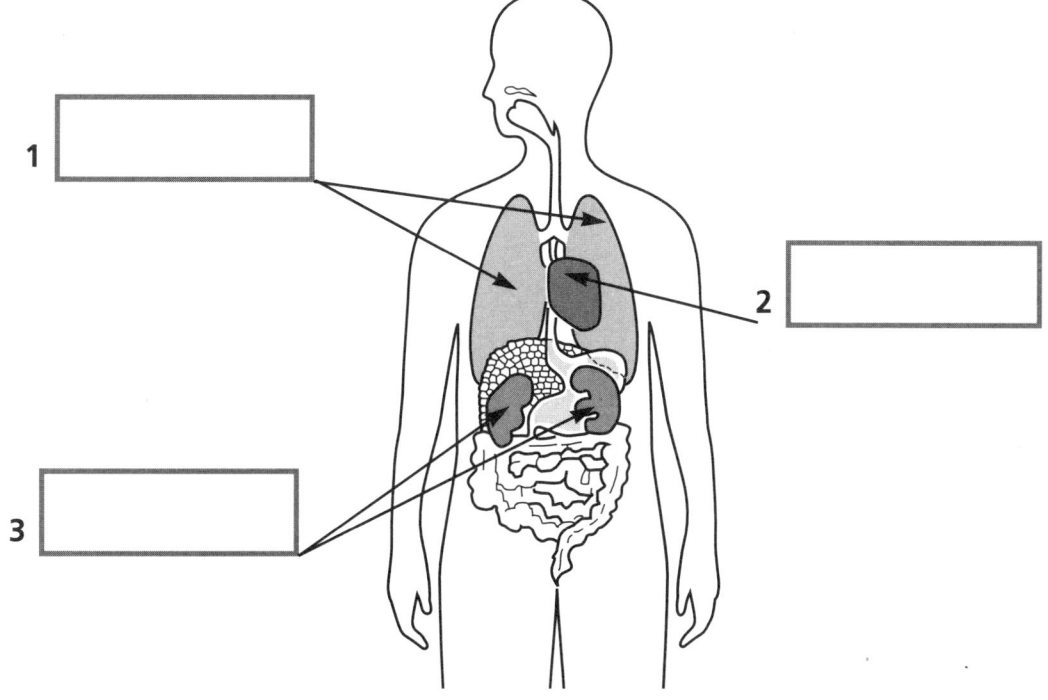

1
2
3

a) Name the **three** organs marked in the diagram. Use the words written in the box above.

b) What does the **heart do to the blood**?
_____

c) What do the **kidneys do to the blood**?
_____

d) What happens to the **blood in the lungs**?
_____
_____

Test A — Human Body

Each time after doing 4 different activities, Tim waited 3 minutes and then measured his pulse rate.

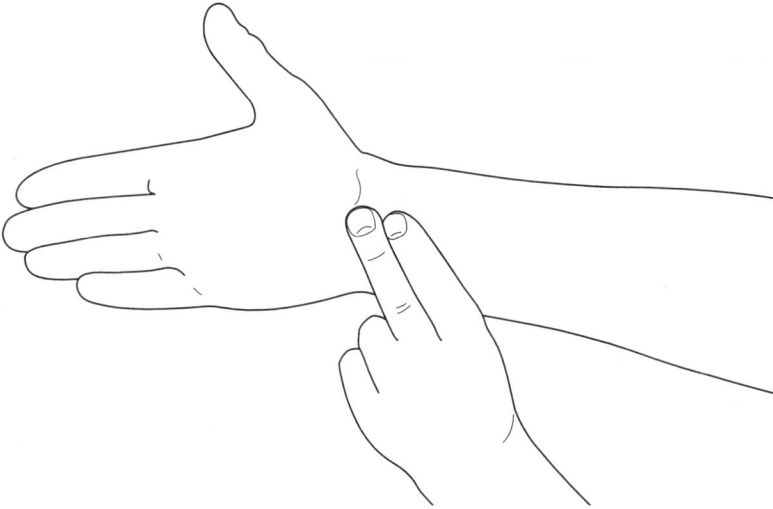

70   **80**   **110**   **130**

e) Fill in the table, putting the **pulse rates** in the **correct places**.

Activity	Pulse rate (heartbeat per minute)
Running on the spot	
Lying down	
Walking on the spot	
Sitting writing	

4

total

Pond Life

The pond in the picture has many plants and animals living in it. Some are shown here.

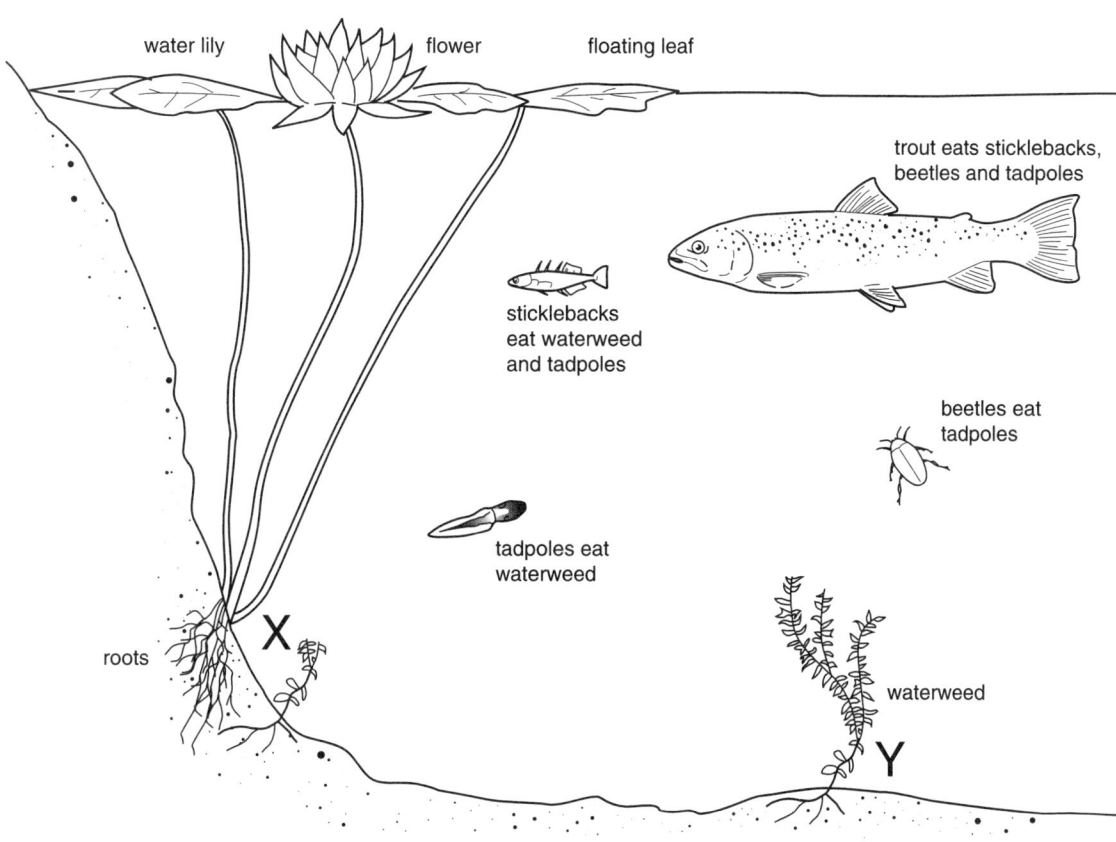

a) Tick the box below which explains why the **waterweed grows better at Y than at X.**

☐ The waterweed gets more nutrients at Y.

☐ The waterweed has more room at Y.

☐ The waterweed gets more light at Y.

Test A — Pond Life

b) Name a **predator** in the pond shown on page 9.

_____

c) Name a **producer** in the pond.

_____

d) Give **one** example of a **consumer eating another consumer** in the pond.

_____

Fish have **gills** so that they can breathe under water.

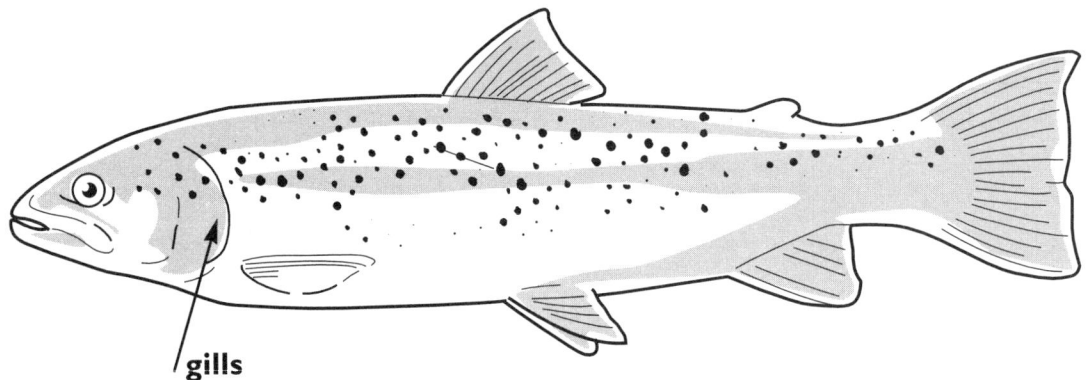

e) Give **another way** that fish are **suited to life in the water**.

_____

_____

Identifying Animals

6

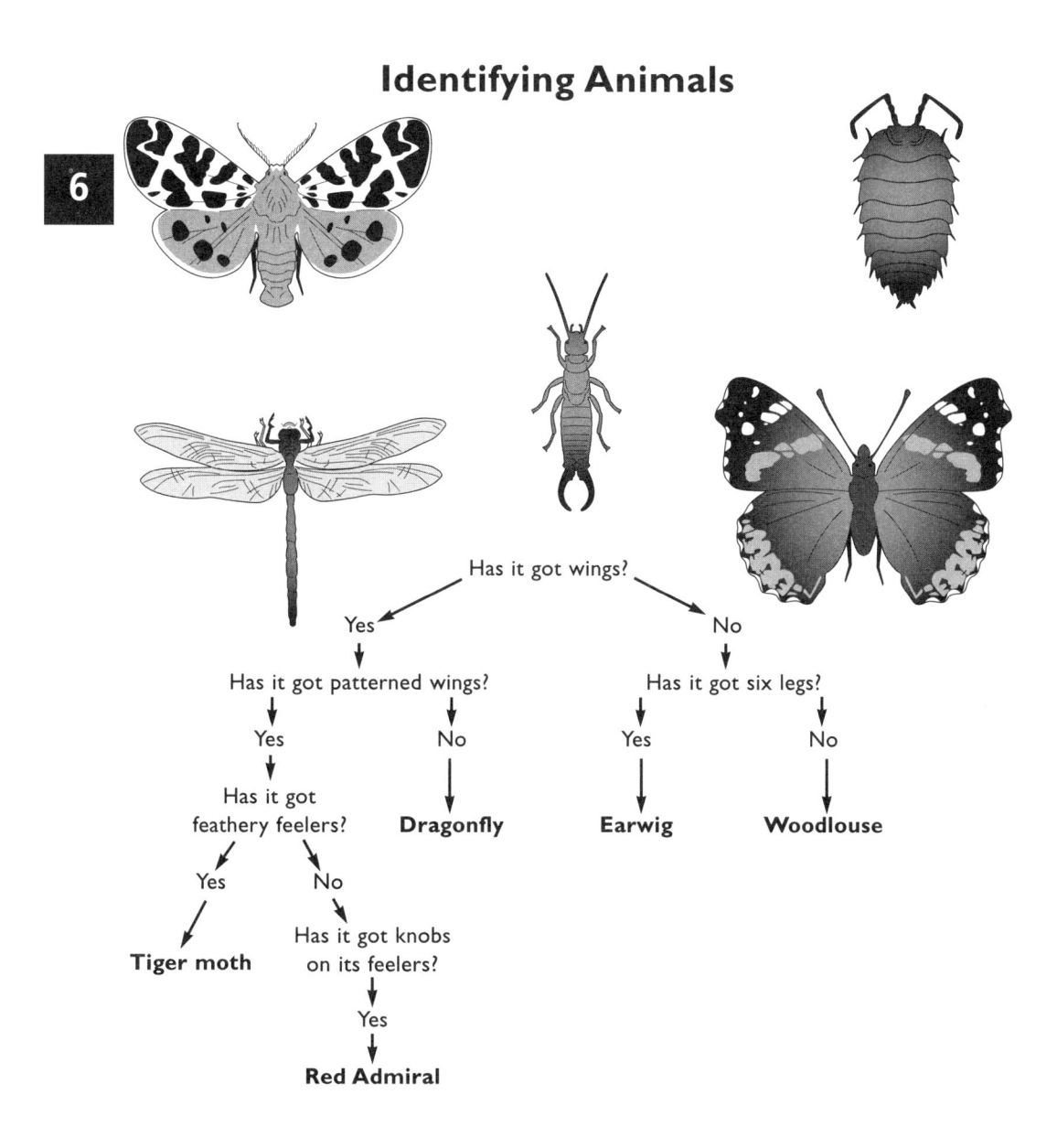

Identify the following animals. **Use the key.**

a) It has **patterned wings** and **feathery feelers**.

_____

b) It has **6 legs** and **does not fly**.

_____

c) It has **patterned wings** but **does not have feathery feelers**.

_____

Flying

7

This aeroplane can fly. It uses **fuel** to power its engine.

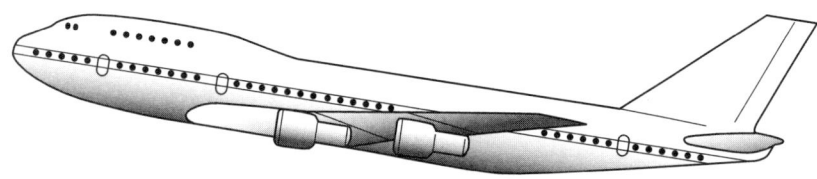

a) What **happens to the fuel** when the aeroplane flies?

_____

_____

1

b) Tick **one** box below to show that **when the energy has been released from all the fuel**:

the fuel is just the same. ☐

waste gases are left. ☐

all the fuel has been changed into water. ☐

all the fuel has been changed into air. ☐

1

The outer body of the aeroplane is made of **Aluminium**.

c) Tick **one** box below to show that **the main reason for using Aluminium**, is because it:

is strong. ☐

is light. ☐

is a metal. ☐

is expensive. ☐

1

total

12

Floating and Sinking

8

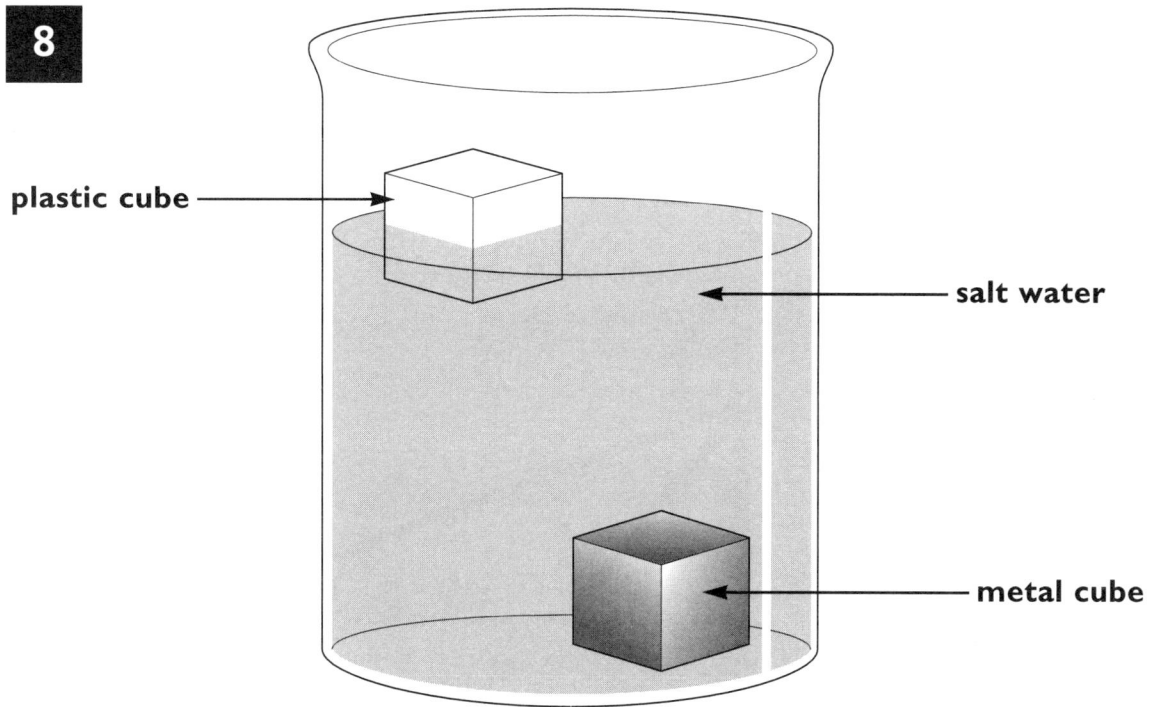

Two cubes of the same size were put into water as shown above.

a) **Show in the diagram** the forces acting on the plastic cube.

b) What would happen to the plastic cube if it were put into **tap water**?

_____

_____

Sun and Light

9

Some children drew and measured the length of shadows at different times on a sunny day.

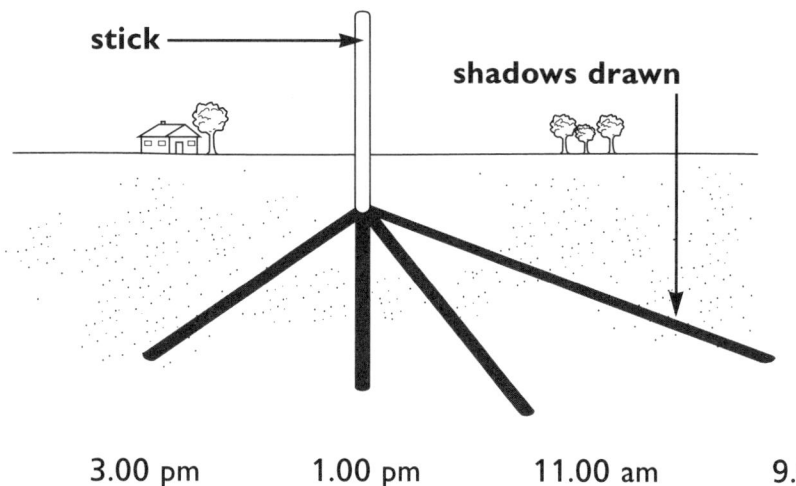

3.00 pm   1.00 pm   11.00 am   9.00 am

a) **Draw** on the diagram the shadow formed at **5.00 pm**.

b) **Why** is the **shadow shorter** at **1.00 pm**?
_____
_____

c) **Why** does the **shadow** of the stick **move**?
_____
_____

d) **Why** does the **stick form a shadow** on a sunny day?
_____
_____

e) If the day were **cloudy, what would happen** to the **shadows**?
_____
_____

Electricity

10

Raj was experimenting with batteries and bulbs. He made up a circuit like this:

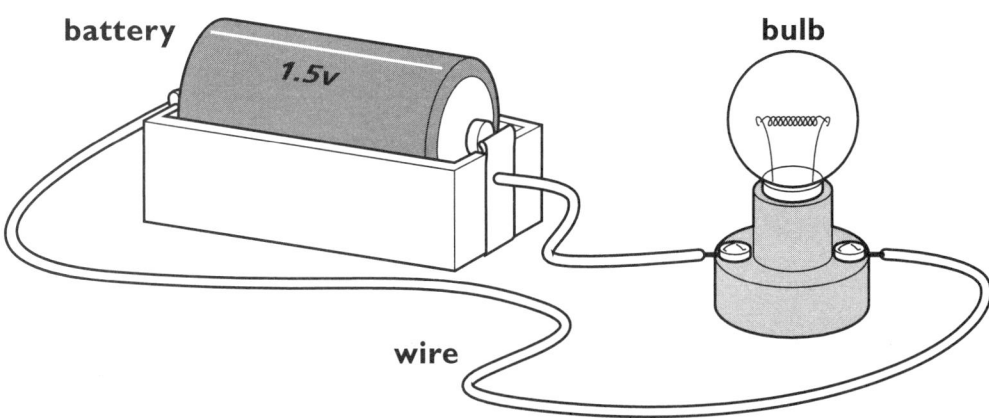

This is the **circuit diagram** to show what Raj did:

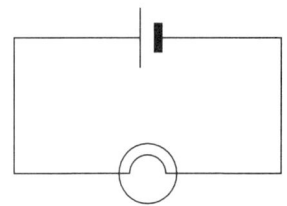

Circuit 1

He wanted a **brighter light** and tried **these circuits**:

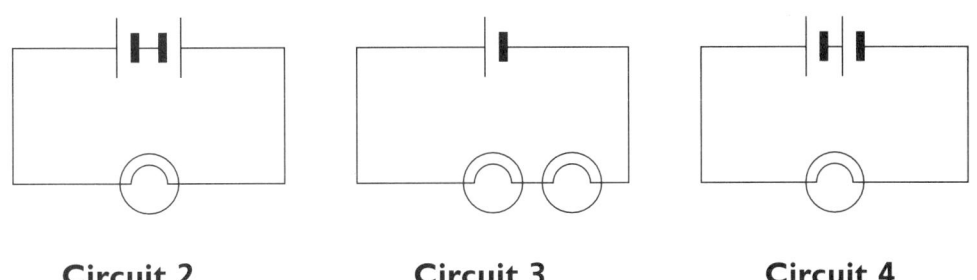

Circuit 2   Circuit 3   Circuit 4

a) Which was the circuit which made the brightest light?

_____

1

Test A — Electricity

Next, Raj wanted to turn his bulb in **Circuit 1, on and off**. He made a **switch**. It looked like this:

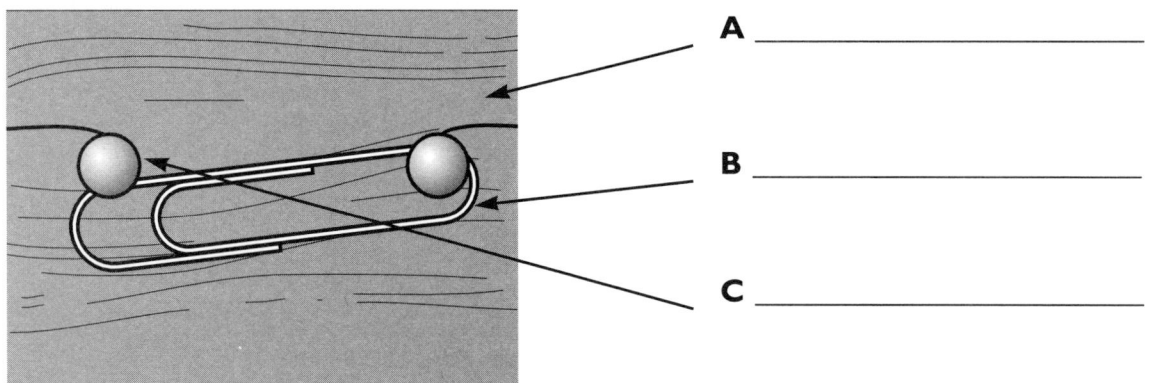

A _____

B _____

C _____

b) **Label the materials** marked on the switch.

c) **Draw a circuit diagram** to **show** how he used the **switch** to turn the **bulb on** and **off**.

Use these symbols:

battery   bulb   switch   connecting wires

Draw here

Test B

Living Things

1

seaweed   grass   human

 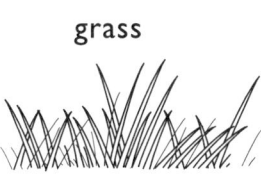 

fish   bird    ant

Tick three boxes only, to show which **three** things, are true of **all living things**.

☐ They grow.

☐ They eat.

☐ They move from place to place.

☐ They need water.

☐ They reproduce.

☐ They sleep.

17

Test B — Flowering Plants

Flowering Plants

2

a) Name the **parts** of the plant (1–4), using **words from inside the box**.

| leaf | sepals | veins | roots | fruit | stalk | petals | seeds |

1 _____

2 _____

3 _____

4 _____

Flowering Plants Test B

- attracts insects needed for pollination

- takes in water for the plant

- protects the developing flower

- has seeds in it which will grow into new plants

- supports the plant

- makes food for the plant

b) Fill in the chart and say what job each part does, **choosing from the statements** above.

Label	Name	Job done by each part
1		
2		
3		
4		

Separating Substances

3

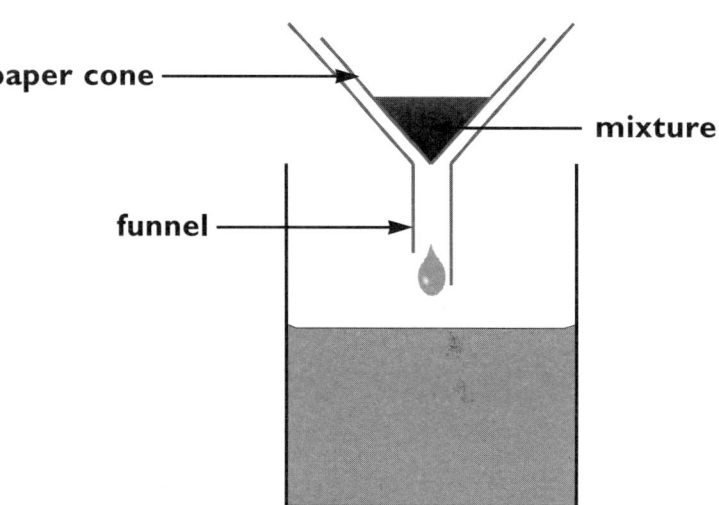

This apparatus could be used to separate substances.

a) **Tick one** box to show which of the **mixtures** can be **separated** using this apparatus.

☐ sugar and salt

☐ sand and water

☐ salt dissolved in water

☐ sugar and salt dissolved in water

b) What is the method of separation shown in the picture called?

_____

Forces

4

Some children were testing how good the grip on shoes was, using a ramp.
The ramp was raised until the shoes just started to move.

a) Name the **force** which **caused the shoes to move**.

_____

b) Name the **force** which **stopped the shoes from moving**.

_____

Their findings were recorded on a chart.

Shoes tested	Height ramp was raised before shoe started to move
trainers	15 cms
sandals	8 cms
rubber boots	10 cms
walking boots	20 cms

c) Which shoes did the children find had the **best grip**?

_____

d) Which shoes **slipped the easiest** on the ramp?

_____

Powders

5

James tested **4** different powders to see if they would dissolve in water.
He added the same amount of powder and water each time.

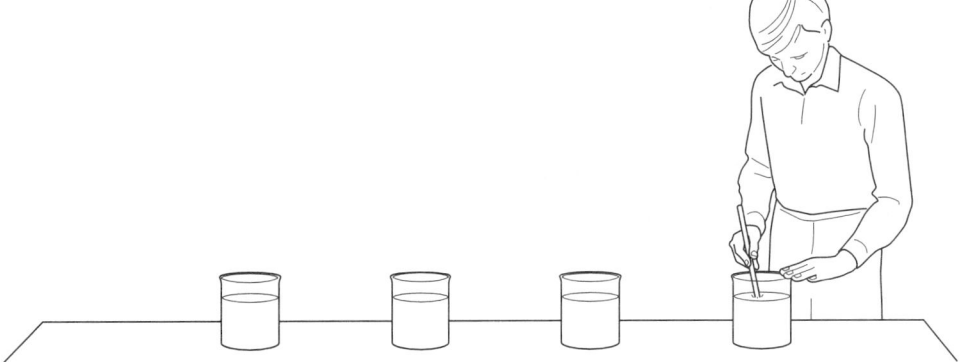

The chart shows his results.

Powder	After stirring for **1** minute in cold water
flour	lumpy, white and cloudy
sugar	clear and colourless
angel delight	lumpy, pink and cloudy
salt	clear and colourless

a) Name a **powder** which made a **solution** in water.

_____

1

b) Name a **powder** which **did not dissolve** in water.

_____

1

c) If you repeated the investigation with hot water, give **one** difference you would expect to see.

_____

1

total

Light

6

It is a sunny day. Nick is using sunlight to signal to his friend, Peter, in the valley below.

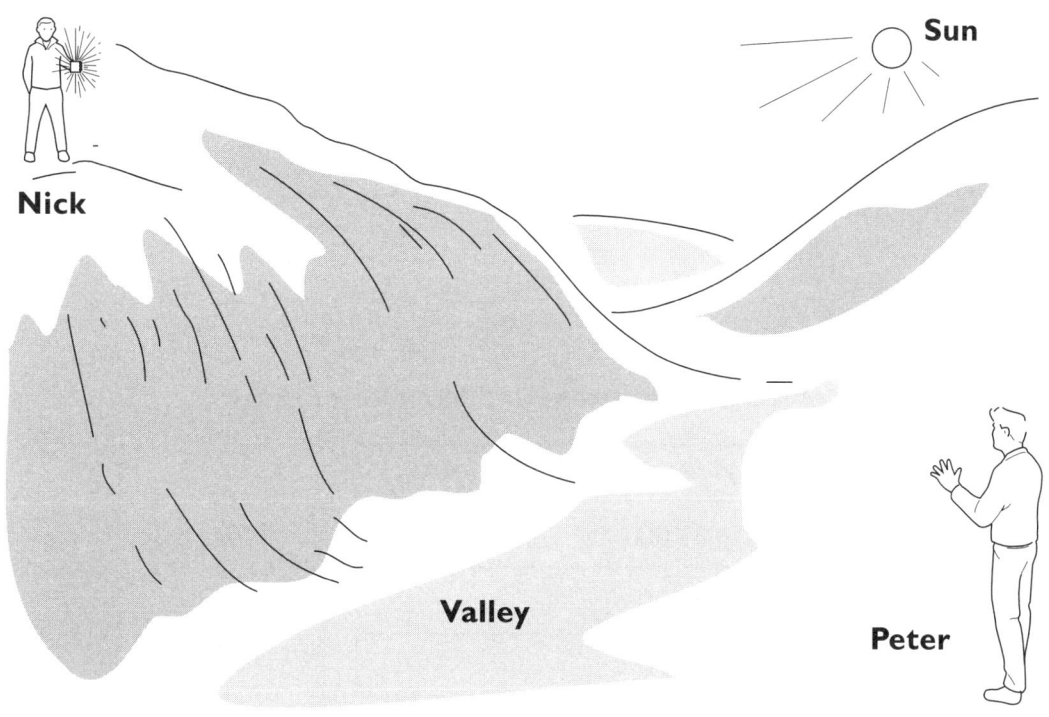

a) Show in the picture, how the sunlight allows Peter to see the signals.

b) **What object** could be **used to send** these signals?
_____

c) What does **this object do** to the sunlight?
_____

d) **At night time**, what could James have used to signal to Peter in the valley?
_____

Healthy Eating

7

We need food like this to give us energy, to grow and be healthy.

The chart shows the energy values of some foods eaten by children for breakfast.

Food	Energy in kJ given by **100g** of food
sugar	1700
milk	1280
cornflakes	1520

a) Which of these foods is most likely to **cause tooth decay**?

_____

b) Suggest **two** ways (1) and (2) children could **prevent** tooth decay.

1) _____

2) _____

c) Which of the 3 breakfast foods would be the **best source of protein**?

_____

Healthy Eating — Test B

Cornflakes are stored **dry** in boxes and keep a long time in a cupboard. Milk has to be stored in a **refrigerator** and only keeps a few days. **An unfinished bowl of cornflakes and milk does not keep very long**.

d) Why is this?

_____

_____

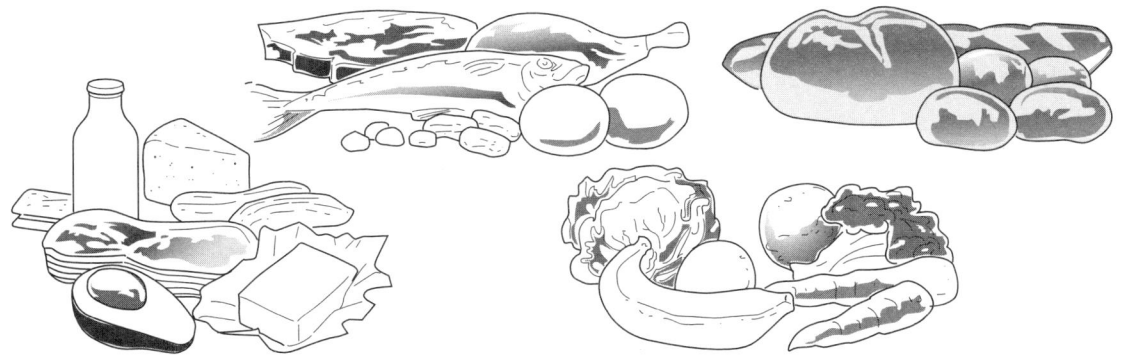

A balanced diet contains a **variety** of foods which provide **nutrients and energy**.

e) Suggest **something other than food** which children need to **stay healthy**.

_____

_____

1

1

total

25

Test B — Drying Clothes

Drying Clothes

On a cold winter's day, some pupils set up an investigation to find the **best place to dry clothes**. 4 pieces of cloth, **all the same size**, were soaked in water then put in different places to find out how long they took to dry. The places chosen were:

 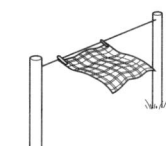 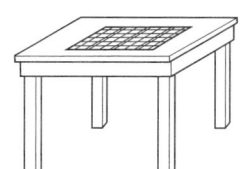 

hanging inside   hanging up outside   flat on a table   in a plastic bag

After 2 hours, they felt how wet each cloth was and their results are shown in the chart below:

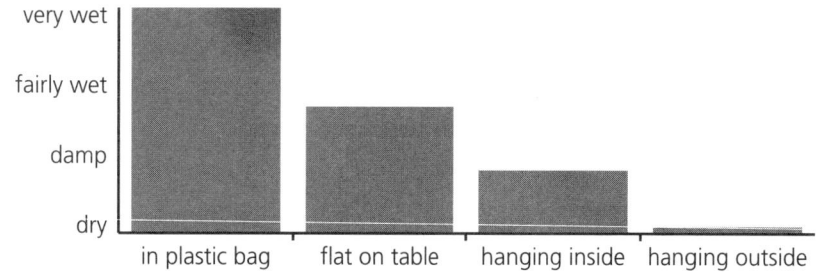

a) **Where** did they find the **best place for drying clothes** was?

_____

b) **Why** did the **cloth in the plastic bag** stay very wet?

_____

_____

c) **What happens to water** on the clothes when they dry?

_____

d) If the investigation had been done on a **hot, dry summer's day, what difference** in the results for the **cloth hanging outside** would be expected?

_____

1

1

1

1

total

Household Waste

9

Many different materials are used in the house. It is important that we recycle as much material as possible to save energy.

a) **Which** of the **waste materials** would you expect to **rot**?

_____

b) How could the **steel objects** be **separated** from the rest of the waste?

_____

c) What is the **raw material** that **paper** is made of?

_____

d) What is the **raw material** that **plastic** is made of?

_____

e) Give **one** reason **why plastic is used** so much for making bottles.

_____
_____

Test B — Cooling Investigation

Cooling Investigation

10

Some children were investigating the cooling of hot water in beakers on a bench in a classroom kept at 18°C. Equal quantities of hot water at 60°C were put into two beakers, A and B.
An ice cube was then put into beaker B.

Beaker A

Beaker B

The children measured the temperature of the water in each beaker every 5 minutes.

a) Draw an ice cube in beaker B to show what it looked like at the beginning of the investigation.

1

b) What happened to the ice cube during the investigation?

_____

1

The graph below shows how the water cooled in **beaker A in 60 minutes**.

c) Draw an approximate curve on the graph to show how the **water cooled in beaker B.**

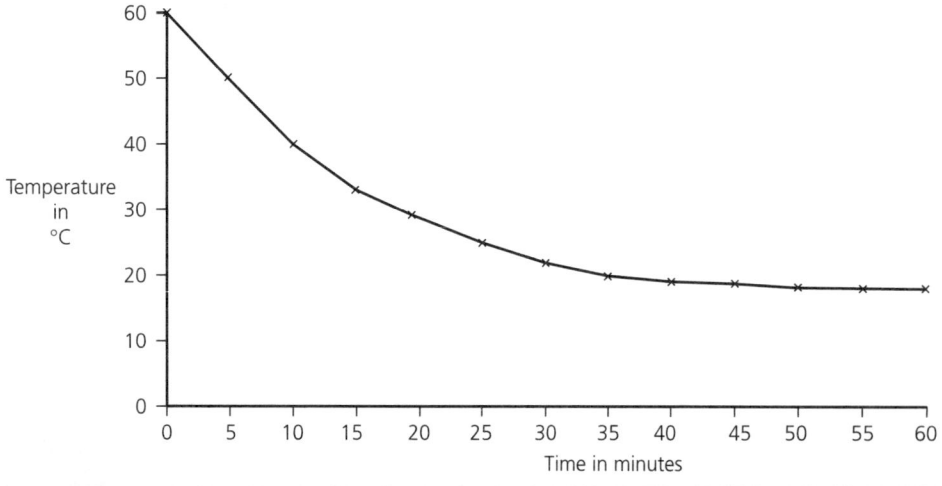

1

total

28

Equal quantities of water at 60°C were put into each beaker.

d) Say **one more** thing that the children should have done to make sure their investigation was **fair**.

1

The beakers were left side by side on the bench until the next day.

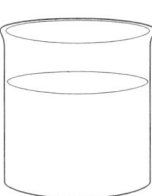

Beaker A ______ **Beaker B** ______

e) Write on the lines above, the **temperature of the water in each beaker** the **following day.**

1

total

Answers Test A — Materials, Magnets, Sound

1

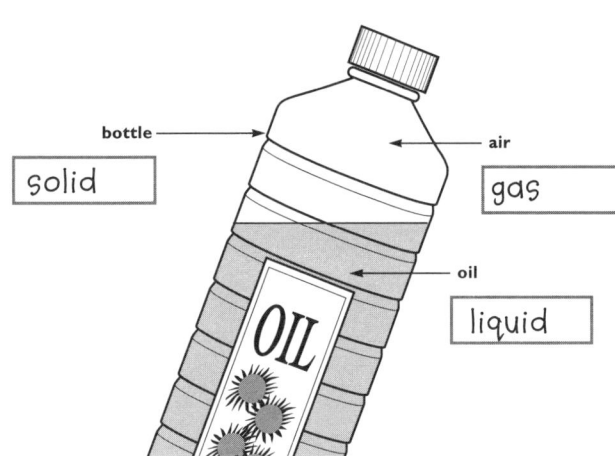

Labels: bottle — solid; air — gas; oil — liquid

A gas fills any space it is in and can be **any** shape.

Solids have a **definite** shape.

Liquids take the shape of the container they are in, but the surface is **always** horizontal.

2 a) ✓ Magnetism.

Magnetism is an invisible force which affects mainly **iron** objects.

b) ✓ They repel (push apart).

When two magnets are put together, **like poles** (ends) **repel** each other, and **unlike poles attract** each other.

c) ✓ The ends are the same, so the magnets repel.

If the magnets are put together and the ends are the same thy will not attract. If two magnets with different ends are put together they will attract one another.

d) ✓ Steel can.

You should **know** that iron and steel are the **only** common metals attracted to magnets.

3 a) ✓ The strings vibrate.

Something has to move (vibrate) for a sound to be made. **Some** vibrations **are so slow**, humans cannot hear the sound; **others** are **so fast, they** also **cannot be heard**. It is important to realise that sounds travel through air, liquids and solids.

b) ✓ The thickest string.

Long, thick strings vibrate **slowly** and so make low sounds (notes). **Short, thin** strings, on the other hand, vibrate much **faster**, so the sounds would be higher.

c) ✓ Tighten the string by turning the peg at the end.

or

✓ Make the string shorter by pressing fingers down.

Either of these is correct for one mark.

Human Body — Answers Test A

4 a)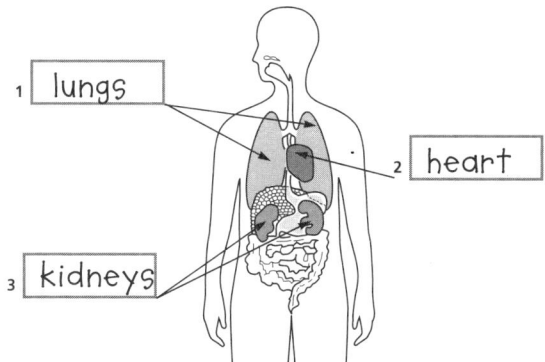

1. lungs
2. heart
3. kidneys

Choose your answers from the organs **listed in the question**, only!
Look carefully at the ends of the arrows to make sure which organ is being indicated.
You should **know** the main organs of the body, where they are located and what their job is.

b) ✓ The heart pumps the blood around the body.

The main point here is that the heart acts like a **pump**. This word is important.

c) ✓ The kidneys filter the blood.
✓ The kidneys remove waste products from the blood.
✓ The kidneys keep the concentration of some substances in the blood, the same (constant).

Any one of these for one mark:

d) ✓ Waste gases, like carbon dioxide and water from the blood, go into the air and oxygen, from the air, goes into the blood.

Note that you are being asked what happens to the **blood.** So in your answer you refer to the blood to get a mark.

e)

Activity	Pulse rate (heartbeat per minute)
Running on the spot	130
Lying down	70
Walking on the spot	110
Sitting writing	80

Remember that your pulse rate goes **up** with more **strenuous exercise.** When you are **resting** the pulse rate is **lower.**

Answers Test A | **Pond Life**

5 **a)** ✓ Gets more light at Y.

The plant at **X** would **not** get much light because the large water lily leaves are floating on the surface of the pond and **cutting out** a lot of light below them. Without light the plant would not be able to **photosynthesise** (make food). Without being able to make food it would die, whether it had plenty of room, or not.

b) ✓ Trout.
✓ Stickleback.
✓ Beetle.

Any one of these for one mark.

Remember that a **predator** is an animal that eats another **animal.**

c) ✓ Waterweed.
✓ Water lily.

Either of these for one mark.

Remember a **producer** is **always** a plant and is always **at the bottom of the food chain.**

d) ✓ Beetles eating tadpoles.
✓ Sticklebacks eating tadpoles.
✓ Trout eating beetles.
✓ Trout eating sticklebacks.
✓ Trout eating tadpoles.

Any one of these for one mark.

Remember a **consumer** is always an **animal.** You should know about how food chains show the relationship of all living things in a habitat like a pond.

e) ✓ The streamlined shape of the fish helps it move through the water easily.
✓ The fins help the fish manoeuvre easily in the water (go in the direction it wants).

Either of these for one mark.

Note that **how animals are adapted to their environment** is a very important part of the curriculum.

Identifying Animals — Answers Test A

6 a) – c)

> Remember that you are to **choose only from the animals shown**!

> When you have to use a key like this, you always:
> ◆ work down from the **top**
> ◆ follow the questions and answers using **the arrows** to lead you to the next part
> ◆ read instructions **very** carefully.

Identifying Animals

6

Has it got wings?
- Yes → Has it got patterned wings?
  - Yes → Has it got feathery feelers?
    - Yes → **Tiger moth**
    - No → Has it got knobs on its feelers?
      - Yes → **Red Admiral**
  - No → **Dragonfly**
- No → Has it got six legs?
  - Yes → **Earwig**
  - No → **Woodlouse**

Identify the following animals. **Use the key.**

a) It has **patterned wings** and **feathery feelers**.
   tiger moth

b) It has **6 legs** and **does not fly**.
   earwig

c) It has **patterned wings** but **does not have feathery feelers**.
   red admiral

Revision Tip
Note that questions using keys are often tested. Get as much practice as possible, perhaps make up some yourself to test yourself or your friends.

Answers Test A — Flying

7 a) – c)

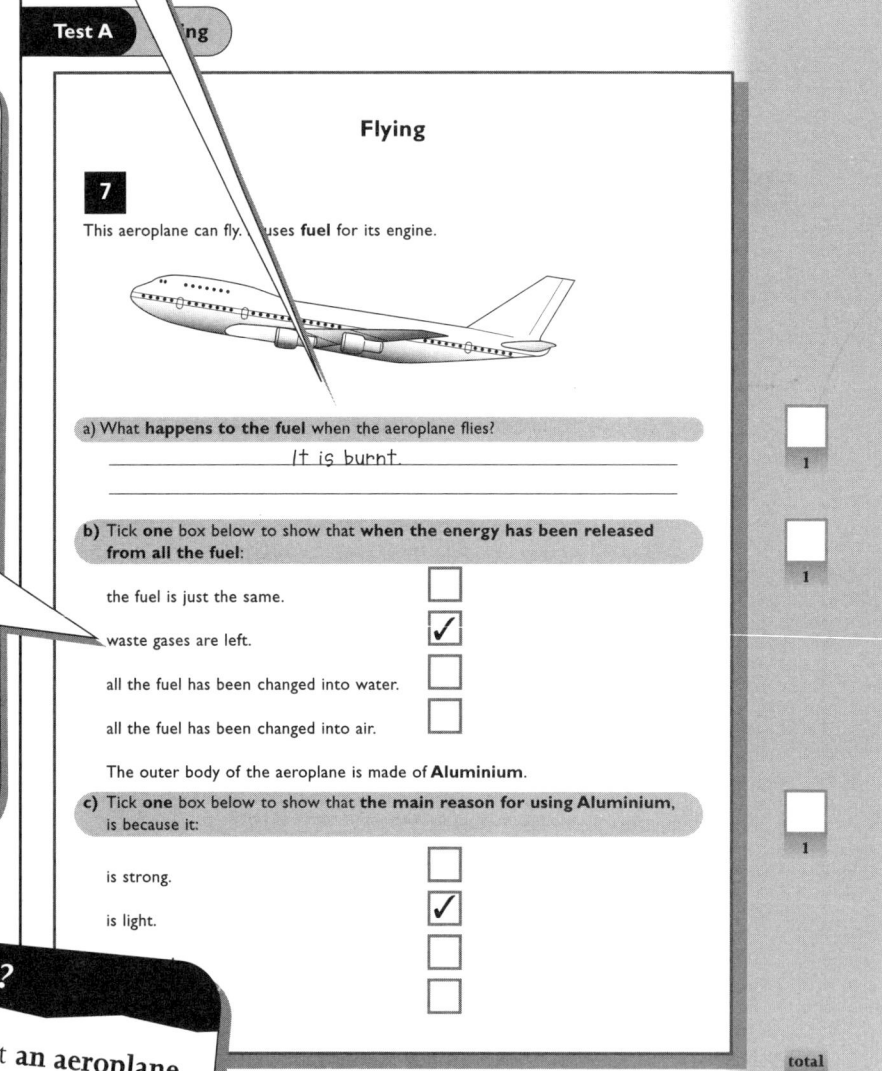

a) Also correct:

The fuel explodes.

b) It is important to know **that burning fuel releases energy and produces waste gases in the process**. The following answers cannot be correct:

◆ **The fuel is just the same.**
It impossible to get energy for nothing, so the fuel must change.

◆ **All the fuel is changed into water.**
Some of the fuel is changed into water when it burns in air, **but not all of it.**

◆ **All the fuel is changed into air.**
Air is a **mixture** of gases. The fuel does not produce this mixture when it burns.

Did you know?

c) The most important thing about **an aeroplane** is that it flies. It must be strong, but it **has to be made of as light a material as possible**. A metal is ideal for the body; it can be beaten into shape and metals are strong. A light metal like Aluminium would be ideal. It would have less weight. Less work therefore needs to be done against gravity to get the plane up into the air. Aluminium is expensive, so we often recycle in order not to waste it. Extracting Aluminium from its natural, raw material, bauxite, is very expensive.

34

Floating and Sinking — **Answers Test A**

8 **a) – b)**

a) You get 1 mark for each of the two forces shown clearly.

Draw **arrows** to depict:

◆ **a downward force**, owing to the cube's weight and gravity

◆ **an upward force** owing to the push of the water up on the cube.

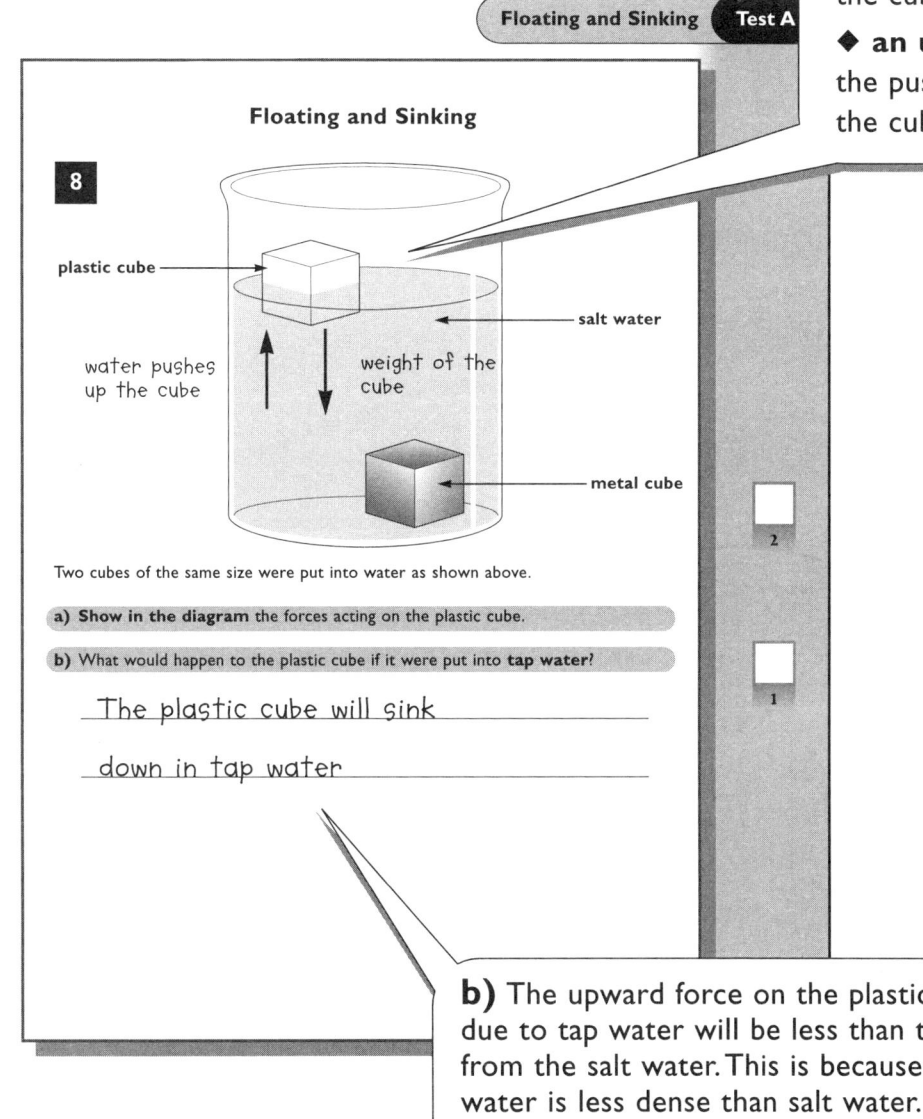

Floating and Sinking — Test A

Floating and Sinking

8

plastic cube
salt water
water pushes up the cube
weight of the cube
metal cube

Two cubes of the same size were put into water as shown above.

a) Show in the diagram the forces acting on the plastic cube.

b) What would happen to the plastic cube if it were put into **tap water**?

   The plastic cube will sink down in tap water

2

1

---

b) The upward force on the plastic cube due to tap water will be less than that from the salt water. This is because tap water is less dense than salt water. The forces on the cube will no longer be balanced. The downward force is now greater, so the plastic cube goes down.

35

9 a) – e)

a) The important points are that:

- **the shadow is longer and,**
- **it has moved further round.**

Draw as carefully as possible

Test A Sun and Light

Sun and Light

...en drew ...d measured the length of shadows at different ... sunny da...

a) **Draw** on the diagram the shadow formed at 5.00 pm.

b) **Why** is the **shadow shorter** at **1.00 pm**?

The Sun is highest in the sky.

c) **Why** does the **shadow** of the stick **move**?

The Earth is turning on its axis. So the shadow seems to move.

d) **Why** does the **stick form a shadow** on a sunny day?

The light cannot pass through the stick.

e) If the day were **cloudy, what would happen** to the **shadows**?

The shadows would not be as dark.

1 1 1 1 1 total

b) Avoid answers like:

- The Sun is the strongest.
- The Sun is on top of the stick.

Simply saying something that may be true, does not mean that you will get a mark. You have to isolate the **important point** - in this case, it is that when a light is very high, short shadows result.

d) Any of the following for one mark:

✓ The stick blocks the light.
✓ The stick is opaque.

Avoid statements like:

- The stick is in the way of the Sun.
- It is because the Sun is behind the stick.

The important point is that a shadow forms when light is stopped by an **opaque object.** Light travels in straight lines. It does not go round objects.

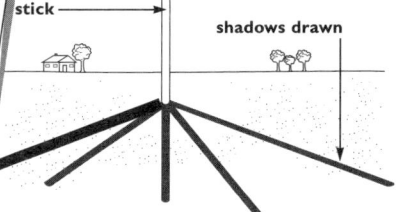

e) Also correct:

✓ The shadows would disappear.

The point here is that you need bright light for sharp shadows. There is still light when it is cloudy, but the light is not as bright. This is because the clouds are translucent (they let the light through).

Electricity   Answers Test A

10 a)

In Circuit 2, there would be no light as the two batteries are not correctly connected so no electricity would flow round the circuit.

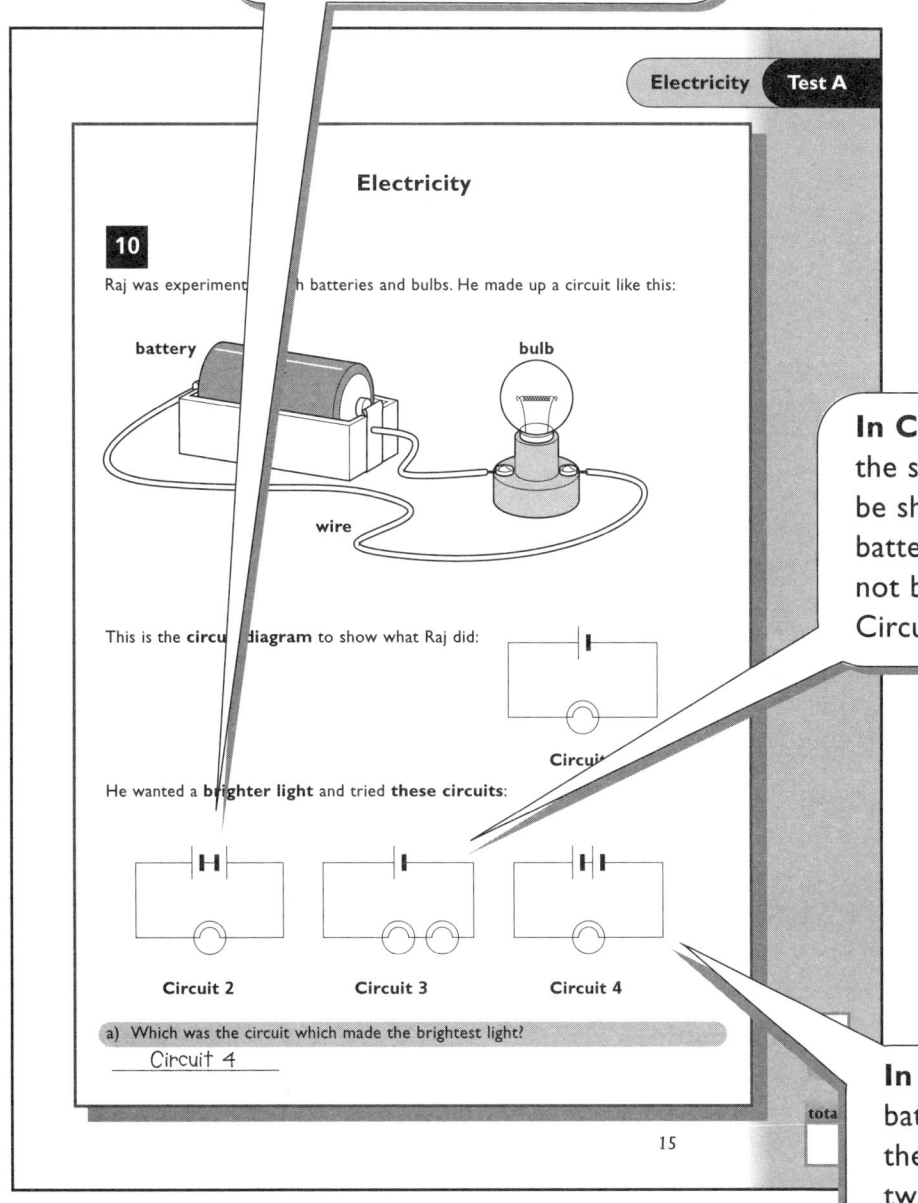

In Circuit 3, two bulbs are in the same circuit, so they would be sharing the energy from the battery. Both therefore, would not be as bright as the bulb in Circuit 1.

In Circuit 4, there are **two** batteries correctly connected in the circuit so there would be twice as much energy and the **bulb would be brighter**.

Electricity   Test A

Electricity

10 Raj was experimenting with batteries and bulbs. He made up a circuit like this:

battery — bulb — wire

This is the **circuit diagram** to show what Raj did:

Circuit 1

He wanted a **brighter light** and tried **these circuits**:

Circuit 2   Circuit 3   Circuit 4

a) Which was the circuit which made the brightest light?
    Circuit 4

Answers Test A — Electricity

10 b) – c)

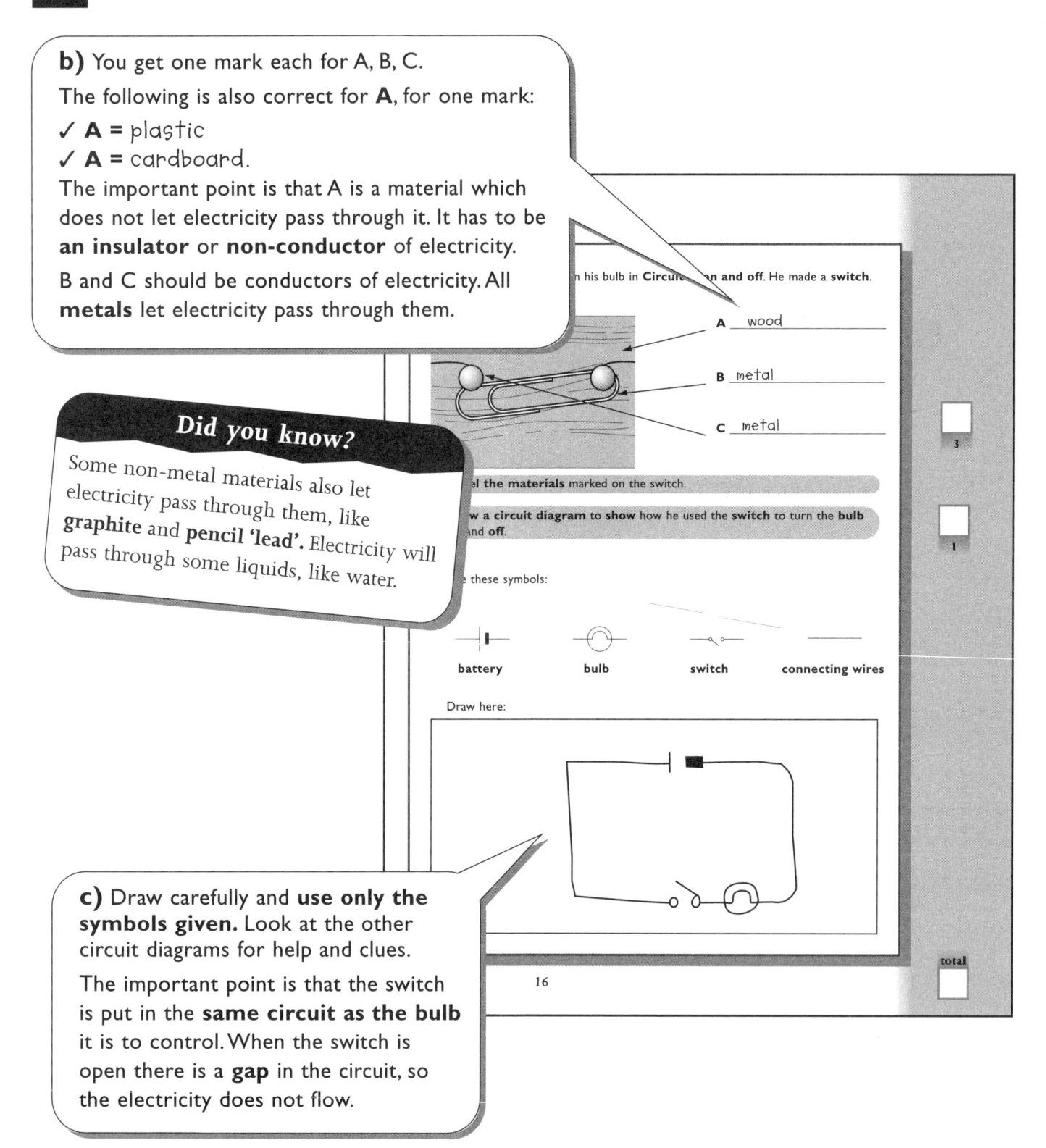

b) You get one mark each for A, B, C.
The following is also correct for **A**, for one mark:
✓ **A** = plastic
✓ **A** = cardboard.
The important point is that A is a material which does not let electricity pass through it. It has to be **an insulator** or **non-conductor** of electricity.
B and C should be conductors of electricity. All **metals** let electricity pass through them.

Did you know?
Some non-metal materials also let electricity pass through them, like **graphite** and **pencil 'lead'**. Electricity will pass through some liquids, like water.

A wood
B metal
C metal

c) Draw carefully and **use only the symbols given.** Look at the other circuit diagrams for help and clues.
The important point is that the switch is put in the **same circuit as the bulb** it is to control. When the switch is open there is a **gap** in the circuit, so the electricity does not flow.

Answers Test B — Living Things

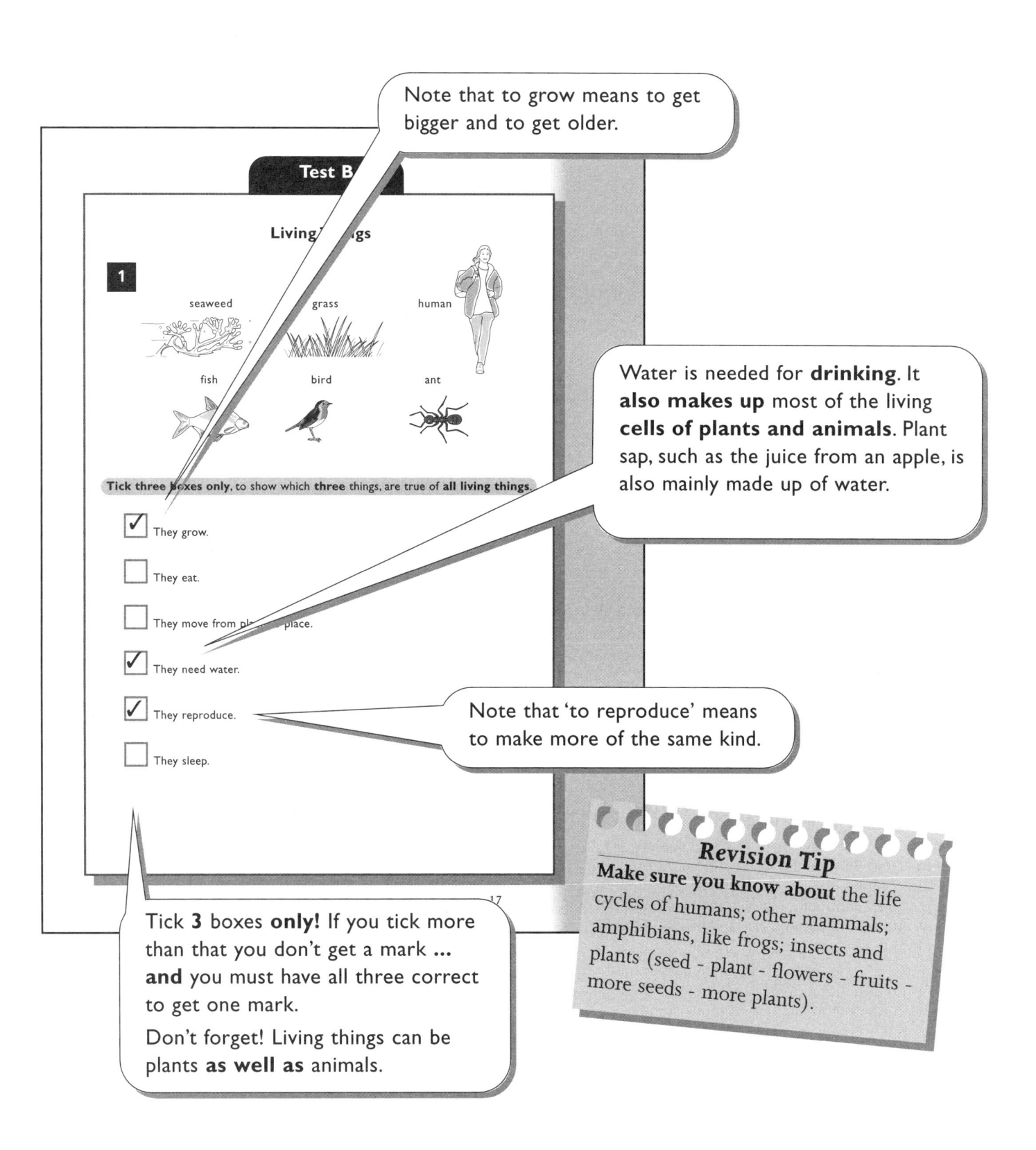

1

Note that to grow means to get bigger and to get older.

Test B

Living Things

1

seaweed grass human
fish bird ant

Tick three boxes only, to show which **three** things, are true of **all living things**.

- ☑ They grow.
- ☐ They eat.
- ☐ They move from place to place.
- ☑ They need water.
- ☑ They reproduce.
- ☐ They sleep.

Water is needed for **drinking**. It **also makes up** most of the living **cells of plants and animals**. Plant sap, such as the juice from an apple, is also mainly made up of water.

Note that 'to reproduce' means to make more of the same kind.

Tick **3** boxes **only**! If you tick more than that you don't get a mark ... **and** you must have all three correct to get one mark.

Don't forget! Living things can be plants **as well as** animals.

Revision Tip
Make sure you know about the life cycles of humans; other mammals; amphibians, like frogs; insects and plants (seed - plant - flowers - fruits - more seeds - more plants).

39

Answers Test B — Flowering Plants, Separating Substances

2 a)

leaf sepals veins roots fruit stalk petals seeds

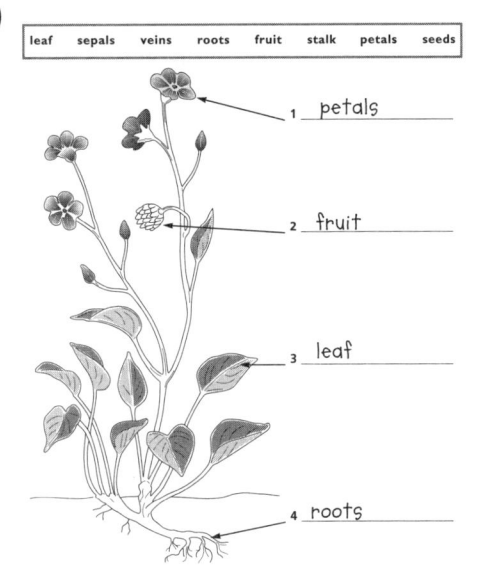

1. petals
2. fruit
3. leaf
4. roots

For answers 1 and 2 look **carefully** at the diagram. You cannot see the individual seeds. The whole seed container seen here is called the fruit (the seeds are inside).

For answer 3 note that the process by which green plants make food using sunlight (photosynthesis) **is a very important part of your studies.**

b)

Label	Name	Job done by each part
1	petals	attracts insects needed for pollination
2	fruit	has seeds in it which will grow into new plants
3	leaf	makes food for the plant
4	roots	takes in water for the plant

You get one mark for each correct point.

You are expected to know the names of the main flowering plants and the jobs done by these parts.

Don't forget! Choose only words from those **shown**.

3 a) ✓ Sand and water.

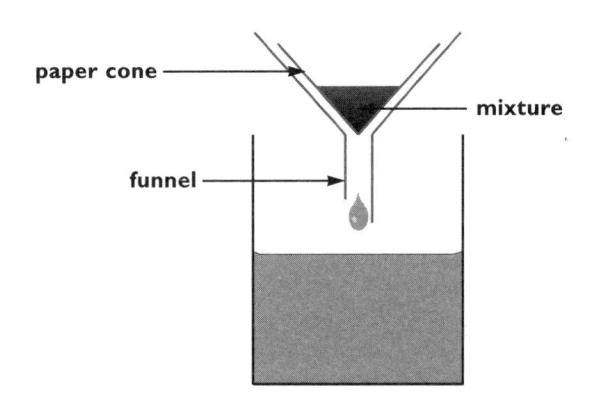

paper cone
mixture
funnel

Look at the chart carefully. Think what each mixture will look like before you answer.

The solid, sand, would be trapped in the paper cone, and the water would be collected in the beaker below. So the mixture would be separated.

Sugar and salt are both solids, so **both** would stay in the paper cone.

Salt dissolved in water would be a liquid **(salt water)** which would go through the paper cone unchanged.

Sugar and salt dissolved in water would be a liquid mixture **(both sugar and salt dissolve in water)** so they would go through the paper cone unchanged.

b) ✓ Filtration or filtering.

You should **know** simple ways to separate mixtures, like pure water from salt water (evaporation), and the pigments in ink (colour chromatography) etc.

… Forces — Answers Test B

4 a) ✓ Gravity.

Gravity pulls things down to the ground. It is probably the most important force in the Universe, responsible for example, for holding the planets in orbit around the Sun.

b) ✓ Friction.

Friction is the force which **stops** two surfaces **moving**. This is sometimes **helpful**. For example when walking, you would need shoe-soles that don't slip.

Lubricants are often used to reduce friction, so:

◆ when sliding - you would need a slippery substance such as snow

◆ when skating - you would need a wet surface

◆ when parts are moving in machinery - grease or oil would be needed.

Their findings were recorded on a chart.

Shoes tested	Height ramp was raised before shoe started to move
trainers	15 cms
sandals	8 cms
rubber boots	10 cms
walking boots	20 cms

c) ✓ Walking boots.

Look for the highest on the chart!

The ramp needs to be raised **20 cms** (highest amount) before the boot starts to move. This shows there was a lot of friction between the boot and the ramp surface.

d) ✓ Sandals.

Look for the lowest on the chart!

The ramp needs to be raised only 8 cms (lowest amount) before the sandal would start to move. This shows there is less friction between the sandal and the ramp surface.

Make sure that you always look at the chart provided, to find your answers.

Answers Test B — Powders

5 a) – c)

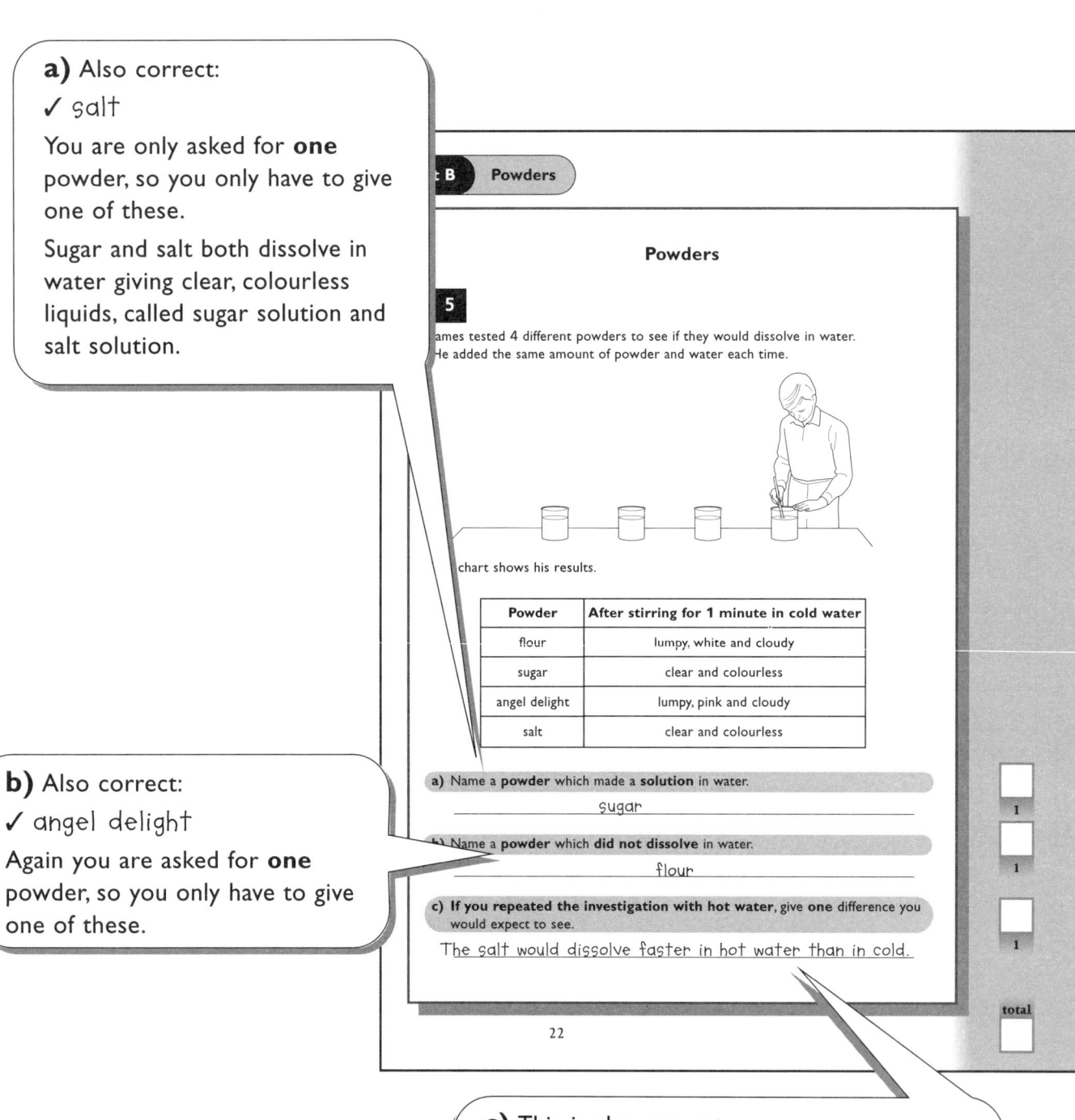

a) Also correct:

✓ salt

You are only asked for **one** powder, so you only have to give one of these.

Sugar and salt both dissolve in water giving clear, colourless liquids, called sugar solution and salt solution.

b) Also correct:

✓ angel delight

Again you are asked for **one** powder, so you only have to give one of these.

c) This is also correct:

✓ The sugar would dissolve faster in hot water than in cold.

Remember that more heat generally makes substances dissolve faster.

Powders

James tested 4 different powders to see if they would dissolve in water. He added the same amount of powder and water each time.

The chart shows his results.

Powder	After stirring for **1** minute in cold water
flour	lumpy, white and cloudy
sugar	clear and colourless
angel delight	lumpy, pink and cloudy
salt	clear and colourless

a) Name a **powder** which made a **solution** in water.
   sugar

b) Name a **powder** which **did not dissolve** in water.
   flour

c) **If you repeated the investigation with hot water**, give **one** difference you would expect to see.
   The salt would dissolve faster in hot water than in cold.

Light — Answers Test B

6 **a) – d)**

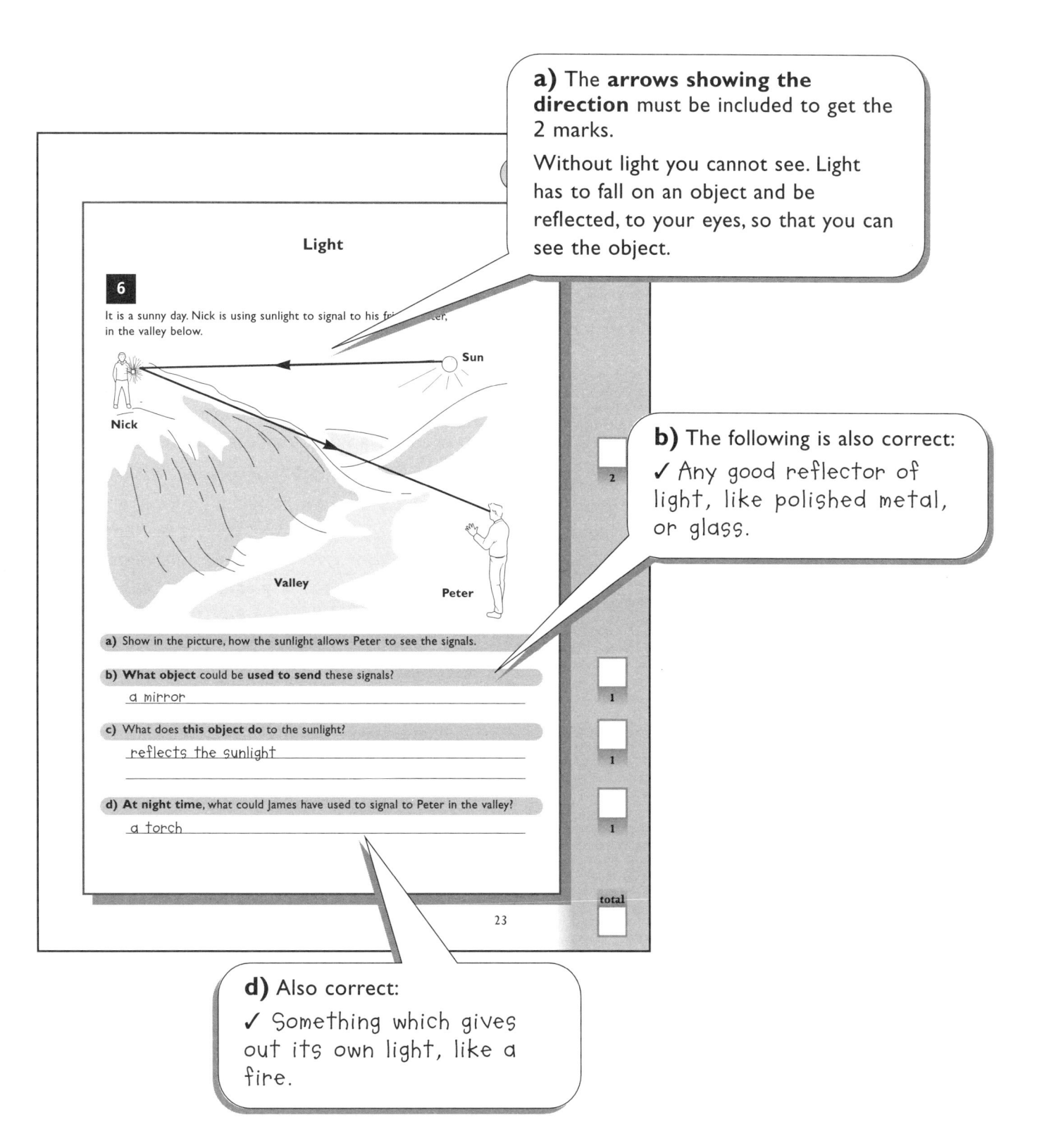

a) The **arrows showing the direction** must be included to get the 2 marks.

Without light you cannot see. Light has to fall on an object and be reflected, to your eyes, so that you can see the object.

b) The following is also correct:
✓ Any good reflector of light, like polished metal, or glass.

d) Also correct:
✓ Something which gives out its own light, like a fire.

Light

6 It is a sunny day. Nick is using sunlight to signal to his friend Peter, in the valley below.

Nick — Sun — Valley — Peter

a) Show in the picture, how the sunlight allows Peter to see the signals.

b) What **object** could be **used to send** these signals?
   a mirror

c) What does **this object do** to the sunlight?
   reflects the sunlight

d) **At night time**, what could James have used to signal to Peter in the valley?
   a torch

43

Answers Test B — Healthy Eating

7 a) ✓ Sugar.

Food	Energy in kJ given by **100g** of food
sugar	1700
milk	1280
cornflakes	1520

Look at the chart! Energy values for the foods are given and they are fairly similar.

You should **know** the main reasons for tooth decay and how to avoid it.

b) ✓ Eat less sugary foods.
✓ Clean teeth regularly.

c) ✓ Milk.

An alternative answer would be:
✓ Visit the dentist regularly.
✓ Use fluoride toothpaste.

You should **know** the **main food groups**, such as proteins, carbohydrates and fats etc., and why they are important for healthy living. We do not just eat food to provide us with energy to do things. Certain chemicals are needed for special processes in the body and we get them by eating particular foods.

d) ✓ Microbes (bacteria) in the air grow in the wet food.

Remember that microbes need moisture to grow. So, we stop food decaying by keeping the food dry and covered to stop microbes getting onto food in the first place. Some 'wet' foods have to be stored at a lower temperature to slow down the growth of microbes in them, like milk.

You also need to **know** that most microbes or bacteria are harmful to us and that there is a need for hygiene.

e) Any one of these is correct for one mark:
✓ Plenty of exercise.
✓ Not to smoke.
✓ Not to take harmful substances.

◆ An **unacceptable** alternative answer is 'taking vitamin tablets,' because if you eat a good variety of foods, the vitamins would be in the foods eaten.

Some chemicals are good for you, like medicines, but others may be harmful.

Drying Clothes, Household Waste — Answers Test B

8

a) ✓ Hanging outside.

There are many different ways the results could be recorded. Make sure you read the chart carefully! The shortest bar = the driest cloth.

b) ✓ No air could get to the cloth, so the air could not evaporate.

You should **know** that air is needed for water to evaporate. **Evaporation** (water changing into water vapour) and **condensation** (water vapour changing back into water) **are very important processes**. They are often tested.

c) ✓ The water evaporates into the air.

Do not use expressions like 'the water disappears.' The water has not disappeared. It has just changed into a gas which is in the air, but the particles are too small for us to see.

d) ✓ The cloth would dry faster.

The important point here is that air is essential for evaporation. On a hot, dry day however, the temperature is higher and there is less water vapour in the air. Evaporation is therefore easier and faster.

9

a) Any one of these is correct for one mark:
- ✓ Carrots.
- ✓ Chicken.
- ✓ Bread.
- ✓ Vegetables.
- ✓ Newspapers.

Remember that all plant and animal material decays (rots) with time.

This question highlights an important use of microbes. They help break down once living material, into useful, rich material that helps make up nutritious soil.

b) ✓ With a magnet.

Steel is an alloy of iron. (It **is** mainly iron.) Only objects with mainly iron in them, are attracted to magnets.

c) ✓ Wood.

d) ✓ Oil.

Note that plastic is a man-made material made from chemicals which are made from oil.

e) Any one of these is correct for one mark:
- ✓ It easy to mould into different shapes.
- ✓ It is quite strong in certain shapes.
- ✓ It is quite cheap to make.

The difference between natural and man-made materials is important. So is the fact that many new materials can be made from natural materials, although the processes may be different or expensive.

Answers Test B — Cooling Investigation

10 a) – c)

a) Draw clearly, and show that the ice cube floats in the water at the surface. This shows that the ice is slightly less dense and lighter than the water.

b) You should **know** the difference between 'melting' and 'dissolving', both of which are often confused by pupils.

c) The line drawn should show a faster rate of cooling. The line should never be higher than the original line, and should start at the same point as that for Beaker A.

The ice cube will obviously make the water colder faster in B, but the temperature will never be lower than that of the room unless a very large ice cube is used. The final temperature would still be about 18°C.

Cooling Investigation

10 Some children were investigating the cooling of hot water in beakers on a bench in a classroom kept at 18°C. Equal quantities of hot water at 60°C were put into two beakers, A and B.
An ice cube was then put into beaker B.

Beaker A   Beaker B

The children measured the temperature of the water in each beaker every 5 minutes.

a) **Draw an ice cube in beaker B** to show what it looked like at the beginning of the investigation.

b) What happened to the ice cube during the investigation?
_____it melts_____

The graph below shows how the water cooled in **beaker A in 60 minutes**.

c) **Draw a line on the graph** to show how the water cooled in beaker B.

46

Cooling Investigation — Answers Test B

10 d) – e)

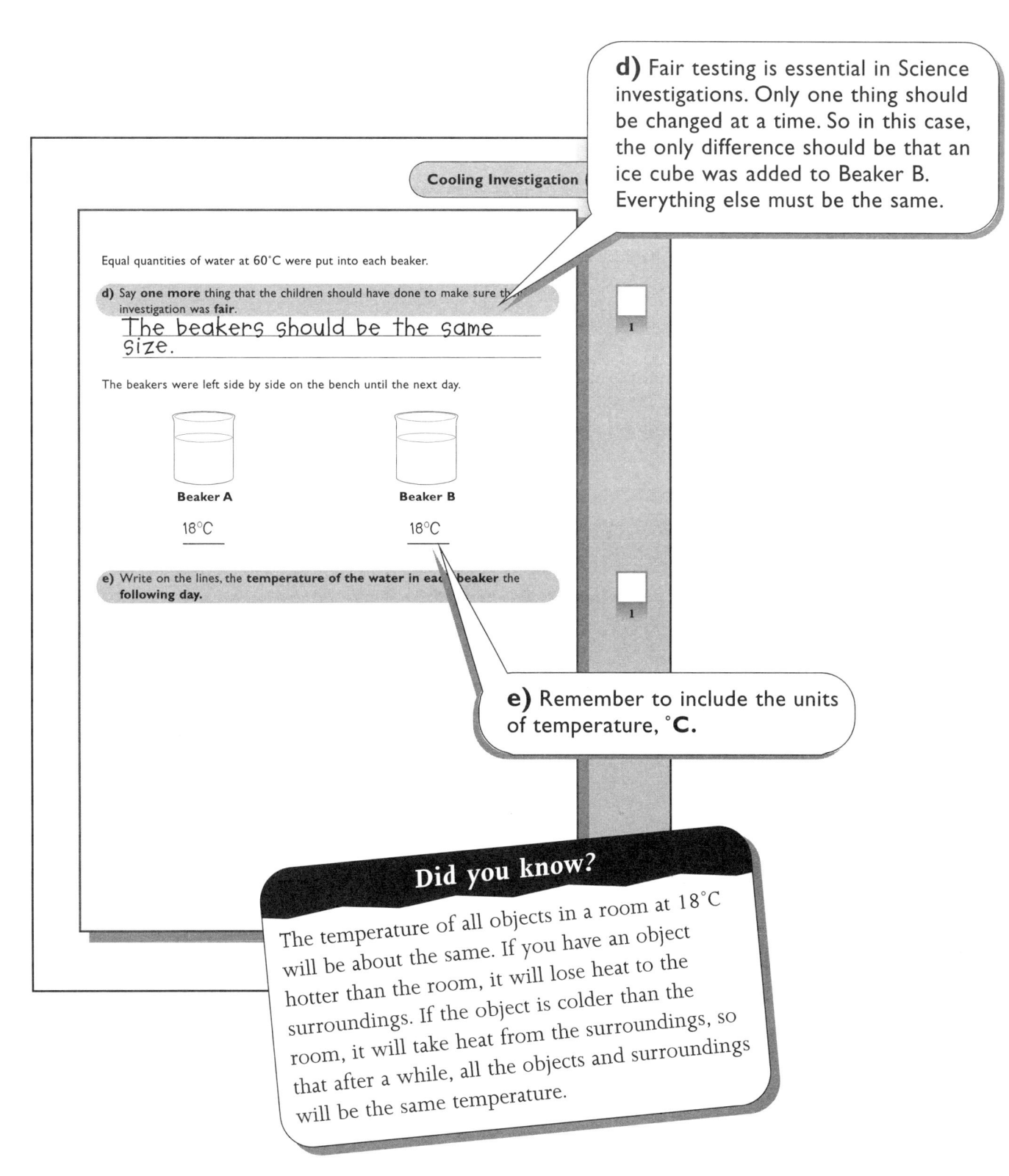

d) Fair testing is essential in Science investigations. Only one thing should be changed at a time. So in this case, the only difference should be that an ice cube was added to Beaker B. Everything else must be the same.

Equal quantities of water at 60°C were put into each beaker.

d) Say **one more** thing that the children should have done to make sure the investigation was **fair**.

The beakers should be the same size.

The beakers were left side by side on the bench until the next day.

Beaker A   Beaker B
18°C   18°C

e) Write on the lines, the **temperature of the water in each beaker** the following day.

e) Remember to include the units of temperature, °C.

Did you know?

The temperature of all objects in a room at 18°C will be about the same. If you have an object hotter than the room, it will lose heat to the surroundings. If the object is colder than the room, it will take heat from the surroundings, so that after a while, all the objects and surroundings will be the same temperature.

Marks, Scores and Levels

Marking the test

Do not penalise incorrect spelling.

Using the marking grid

Make a note of the marks scored, on grids A and B below.

Add together the total number of marks awarded for Test A and Test B.
Find the level by comparing your child's mark with the corresponding level in the chart below.

Total marks	National comparison for age group
20 -22	Your child has not had enough experience in Science.
23 - 44	Working at level 3
45 - 63	Working at level 4
63 or above	Working at least at level 5

TEST A		
Question	Marks allocated	Marks scored
1	3	
2	4	
3	3	
4	7	
5	5	
6	3	
7	3	
8	3	
9	5	
10	4	
subtotal	40	

TEST B		
Question	Marks allocated	Marks scored
1	3	
2	4	
3	2	
4	4	
5	3	
6	5	
7	5	
8	4	
9	5	
10	5	
subtotal	40	
TOTAL	80	